PROPERTY OF
WHITE OAKS PUBLIC SCHOOL

BIG BEASTS
Shark

Stephanie Turnbull

Published by Smart Apple Media,
an imprint of Black Rabbit Books
P.O. Box 3263, Mankato, Minnesota, 56002
www.blackrabbitbooks.com

U.S. publication copyright © 2015 Smart Apple Media.
International copyright reserved in all countries.
No part of this book may be reproduced in any form
without written permission from the publisher.

Designed by Hel James
Edited by Mary-Jane Wilkins

Library of Congress Cataloging-in-Publication Data
Turnbull, Stephanie.
 Shark / Stephanie Turnbull.
   pages cm. -- (Big beasts)
 Summary: "Describes the characteristics of Sharks
and their life and habitat"-- Provided by publisher.
 Audience: Grades K to 3.
 Includes index.
 ISBN 978-1-62588-170-0
 1. Sharks--Juvenile literature. I. Title.
 QL638.9.T665 2015
 597.3--dc 3
                              2014003973

Photo acknowledgements
l = left, r = right, t = top, b = bottom
title and page 3 iStockphoto/Thinkstock; 4 FAUP/Shutterstock;
5 Arend van der Walt/Shutterstock; 6 iStockphoto/Thinkstock;
7 James A Dawson/Shutterstock; 8 iStockphoto/Thinkstock;
10 Jupiterimages/Thinkstock; 11 BW Folsom/Shutterstock;
12 davidpstephens/Shutterstock; 13 Mogens Trolle/Shutterstock;
14 melissaf84/Shutterstock; 15 Andrea Leone/Shutterstock;
16 Thinkstock; 17t nicolas.voisin44, b Mark Doherty/both
Shutterstock; 18 Rich Carey/Shutterstock; 19 Ethan Daniels/
Shutterstock; 20 iStockphoto/Thinkstock; 21 Sekundator/
Shutterstock; 22 background iStockphoto/Thinkstock,
inset Patryk Kosmider/Shutterstock; 23 background
Greg Amptman/Shutterstock, l to r Stocksnapper/
Shutterstock, iStockphoto/Thinkstock, Efired/Shutterstock
Cover Rich Carey/Shutterstock

Printed in China

DAD0059
032014
9 8 7 6 5 4 3 2 1

Contents

Sea Monsters   4

Big Bodies   6

Gentle Giants   8

Terrible Teeth   10

Smart Hunters   12

Dinner Time   14

Deadly Weapons   16

Clever Camouflage   18

Eggs and Babies   20

BIG Facts   22

Useful Words   24

Index   24

Some sharks are
gigantic!

Sea Monsters

There are hundreds of different sharks.

Some are small enough to fit in your hands, but others are longer than a bus.

Sharks live in oceans all over the world. Most prefer deep, warm water, but a few sometimes swim near to shore.

Big Bodies

Sharks are fish. They breathe by gulping in water and pushing it out through slits called gills.

Their smooth bodies, slim fins, and strong tails help them power through water.

Oceanic whitetip sharks have extra-long fins that look like aircraft wings.

Gentle Giants

The biggest sharks of all are whale sharks.

Whale sharks are **massive** but they only eat tiny plants and animals called plankton.

They open their huge mouths wide and suck in water and plankton. Water flows out through gills, but plankton is trapped.

Terrible Teeth

Many sharks are deadly predators. Their strong jaws are full of sharp, pointed teeth for spearing slippery fish.

Extra rows of teeth grow behind the front teeth.

When a tooth breaks off, a new one moves forward to replace it.

Some teeth have jagged edges for slicing flesh.

Smart Hunters

Sharks are excellent hunters.
They can smell prey from far away
and sense even the tiniest movements.

They often lurk near fish or seals...

... then suddenly **z o o m** up through the water, snatching at prey with their jaws.

Dinner Time

Sharks usually hunt alone, but hundreds may gather at good feeding places.

They gobble fish whole and take bites out of big animals to see if they're tasty.

Sharks love fatty animals such as seals, dolphins, and even whales. Humans are too bony!

Deadly Weapons

Saw sharks have a long, blade-like snout edged with teeth. It's perfect for slashing at prey like a sword.

16

Thresher sharks have an extra-long tail to *swat* fish.

Hammerheads **bash** prey with their handy hammer!

Clever Camouflage

Sharks have dark, mottled bodies that blend into the ocean.

Their white underside makes them hard to see from below.

Can you see this wobbegong shark?
It lies flat, hidden on the sea bed, sneakily waiting for small fish to swim close.

It is often called a carpet shark because it looks like a patterned carpet.

Eggs and Babies

Many sharks lay l o n g, thin eggs. Babies grow inside then chew their way out.

Some sharks keep eggs inside their body until they hatch.

The first babies to hatch gobble up the other eggs.

Babies are called pups. They make tasty snacks for adult sharks, so they hide until they're bigger.

BIG Facts

Sharks may grow more than 30,000 teeth through their life.

Sharks can even crush the rock-hard shells of large sea turtles.

The largest whale sharks have a mouth big enough to park a car in.

Tiger sharks have a huge appetite. They have been known to eat tires, license plates, baseballs, and oil cans.

23

Useful Words

gills
Breathing holes on the side of a shark's head.

predator
An animal that hunts others to eat.

prey
An animal that is hunted by a predator.

pup
The name for a baby shark.

Index

babies 20, 21
breathing 6
eggs 20, 21
fins 6, 7
gills 6, 9, 24
hunting 12, 13, 14, 15
prey 12, 13, 16, 17, 24
swimming 5, 6
tail 6, 17
teeth 10, 11, 16, 22

Web Link

Visit this web site for great shark facts and photos:
www.kidzone.ws/sharks